How to use these notes

Guided Read

Walkthrough/Bo

A *walkthrough*, or book introduct _____ of
children. During the walkthrough, _____ d
significant vocabulary they will me _____

Go through the whole of the walkthrough before the children start reading
independently. The walkthrough notes on pages 2 and 3 of this booklet provide
prompts for you to use, specific to *Two Baby Elephants*. The questions, comments
and suggestions alert children to ideas and vocabulary they will need in order to
read independently and with full understanding.

Independent Reading *(pages 4–5)*

After doing a walkthrough, ask the children to read the text aloud, on their own, at
their own pace. Observe the strategies each child uses, praising successful problem
solving and expressive reading. Prompts are suggested for good phrasing, use of
word-solving skills, predicting and checking the meaning, and actively monitoring
the implications of the text, on pages 4 and 5.

After Independent Reading/
Returning to the text *(page 6)*

After the children have read the book independently, return to the text as a group
to reinforce teaching points and to check children's understanding. On page 6, there
are quick follow-up ideas for related text, sentence and word level work.

Responding to the text *(pages 6–8)*

It is important to encourage children to give a personal response to the text.
Discussion ideas related to the book are on page 6.

These Teaching Notes also contain group activity ideas on page 7, and a Photocopy
Master on page 8, for use after the guided reading session or in a follow-up literacy
session.

Guided Reading Notes

Walkthrough

Read the title and the back cover blurb with the children. Ask them to predict what the story is about and discuss whether they think it could be based on real life.

As you introduce the text, encourage the children to think about the pattern of rhythm and rhyme. This should support them in their reading of unfamiliar words.

Pages 2–3

PROMPTS (Read these pages aloud to the children, modelling how to read with expression and intonation appropriate to the rhythm.) Do you notice anything about this story? (Prompt for *it rhymes*.) What do you think is going to happen?

One fine day when Mum was away,
two baby elephants came to play.

They ate all the food,
they drank all the drink,
they broke all the dishes
in the kitchen sink.

Continue the walkthrough to page 6, discussing what's happening in the illustrations.

Pages 6–7

PROMPTS (Some words on these pages echo sounds associated with meaning. Tell the children that this is called *onomatopoeia [pronounced on-oh-mat-o-pee-ya].*) What sorts of sounds would you expect to hear if the elephants jumped in the bath? Can you find a word in the text which sounds like its meaning?

With a thump, thump, thump,
and a crash, bang, crash,
they jumped in the bath
with a splish, splosh, splosh.

They scrubbed their backs,
they scrubbed their tails,
they weighed themselves
on the bathroom scales.

Pages 8–9

PROMPTS What have the elephants done? There's water everywhere! The room is flooded!

> They made the towels all black with mud. They made the bath and the toilet flood.

> They put their pyjamas on and went to bed. "Thank you for having us," the elephants said.

Pages 10–11

PROMPTS Oh no! Mum's come home to all the mess. What might she be saying to the little boy and girl? (Prompt for the word *who*.) Praise suggestions that would fit, such as 'Who made all the mess?'

> Mum came home later that day and this is what she had to say:

> "Who ate the food? Who drank the drink? Who broke the dishes in the kitchen sink?

Walk on through to page 14, pointing out that Mum is still talking.

Page 14

PROMPTS What do you think Mum saw when she peeped round the door? What do you think the children said to their mum?

> "It wasn't us!" my brother said. "It was two baby elephants. They're in your bed." Mum peeped round the bedroom door. What do you think that our mum saw?

Ask the children to predict the ending but stop the walkthrough at page 14. Go back to the start of the book and ask the children to read independently.

Before the children begin to read independently remind them to read with intonation and expression appropriate to the pattern of the rhythm.

Pages 4–5

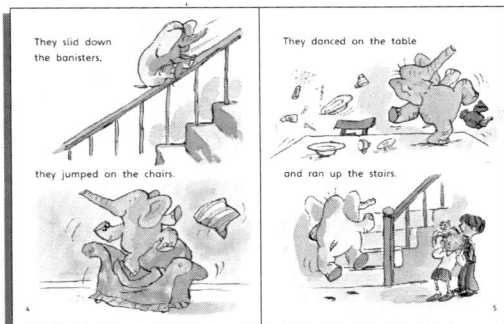

CHECK that the child reads with appropriate pace and rhythm, taking account of the full stops.

Pages 6–7

CHECK that the child reads rhythmically, taking account of the commas.

CHECK for reading of onomatopoeic words.

"Well done. You read that word the way it sounds."

Pages 8–9

> They made the towels
> all black with mud.
> They made the bath
> and the toilet flood.

> They put their pyjamas on
> and went to bed.
> "Thank you for having us."
> the elephants said.

CHECK for accurate reading of *flood*.
"This word rhymes with mud. Try splitting it into two sounds (*fl-ood*)."

CHECK for accurate reading of *pyjamas*.
"Split the word into syllables. What do you wear in bed?"

Pages 12–13

> "Who broke the table?
> Who broke the chairs?
> Who's been running
> up and down the stairs?"

> "Why are the towels
> all black with mud?
> Who made the bath
> and the toilet flood?"

CHECK that the child reads at a lively pace, with attention to rhythm and punctuation.

Ask the child to read on, checking that he or she notices the change of speakers.

Page 16

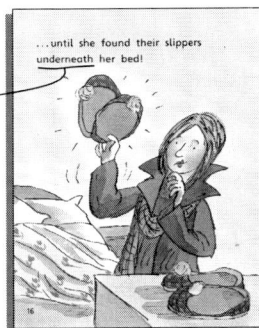

> ...until she found their slippers
> underneath her bed!

underneath
"Look for known words within the word."

5

Word knowledge – consider words with same sounds but different spellings

Ask the children to locate the rhyming words *tails* and *scales* and write them on a flip chart. Ask them to think of other words that rhyme and write these. Draw attention to the different spelling patterns for the vowel phoneme *ai*. The children could then look through the book to find other examples of rhymes, which are spelt differently, for example, *mud/flood (p.8)*, *bed/said (p.9)*, *door/saw (p.14)*.

Sentence knowledge – read familiar texts with expression, raise voice for questions

Ask the children some questions and invite them to comment on the intonation. Tell them to read pages 12 and 13 again, this time concentrating on raising their voices at the end of the questions.

Text knowledge – identify patterns of rhythm, rhyme and other features of sound

Ask the children to read pages 6 and 7 again, concentrating on reading with pace and expression. Let them tap out the rhythm as they read aloud. Discuss how the text is enhanced by the careful choice of words. Discuss the use of onomatopoeia to create sound effects, and ask the children to think of some further examples of onomatopoeic words to write and illustrate.

Responding to the text

- Ask the children what the elephants did.
- Did the children in the story enjoy the visit?
- How do they think Mum felt when she came home? Why?
- Do they think the mess was really made by two baby elephants?

Group activity ideas

❶ Write another verse

AIM to write another verse using the structure of the text and substituting own ideas (*Y2 T1 T12*)

YOU WILL NEED
- flip chart
- pieces of card
- marker pens
- workbooks
- copies of *Two Baby Elephants*

WHAT TO DO Ask the children to suggest what the elephants might have done in the bedroom before they went to sleep. Note their ideas on the flip chart. Reread page 3 together and discuss the pattern and rhyme. Brainstorm words that rhyme with the main words in the children's ideas. They should then write on their cards two sentences about what the elephants did, using rhyming words. When they have done this, demonstrate how to use these ideas to write a verse using the structure of the text, e.g.

They jumped on the bed,
they swung from the light,
they climbed up the curtains,
and had a pillow fight.

Ask the children to use their rhyming sentences to write verses of their own.

❷ Find the phoneme

AIM to read and spell words with long vowel phonemes (*Y1 T3 W1*)

YOU WILL NEED
- pieces of card
- marker pen and highlighter

WHAT TO DO Write words from the text containing long vowel phonemes on separate pieces of card, e.g. *play, peeped, food, home, fine*. Highlight the letters that make the long vowel phoneme. Tell the children to choose a card and write words that contain the same phoneme. The children can search through this text or others for examples.

7

What did Mum say?

Mum came home later that day
and this is what she had to say:

Who drank
the drink?

Ask the children to write down the questions that Mum asked about each of the events
shown in the pictures. Remind them about the use of question marks to indicate
questions. Some children may need a copy of the book for support.

Two Baby Elephants

(NLS: Y1 T3 S7)